Copyright © 1980 by N*I*N Sharyn Bebeau
All rights reserved. Printed in the United States of America.
No portion of this book may be reproduced in any form
without written permission of the author,
except for brief quotations in reviews.

Cover and book design
by N*I*N Sharyn Bebeau

Other Books by N*I*N Sharyn Bebeau M.A.

How to be a Goddess in 28 Days
Weavers of Life — The Archetypes of Soul
Looking Beneath Reality
Meshka the Wise Woman
Meshka and the Goddess

ISBN—13: 9781530646395
ISBN—10: 1530646391

Passover Haggadah
A Celebration of Freedom

N J*N Sharyn Bebeau

Shalom

Shalom means Peace. I wish you peace of mind, peaceful emotions, and a life where you are free and at peace. All this I wish you when I say, "Shalom."

Welcome dear family and guests. It is a joy and an honor to be together on this sacred night. We are here to celebrate Passover, springtime, life, and birth. The Jewish people have celebrated this holiday and the precious gift of freedom every year for over five thousand years.

Tonight, we celebrate springtime, all that is life-giving and joyous. We take this time to rededicate ourselves to living in peace with one another. We are one world bound together. Let our bonds be of love and trust. May torture, enslavement, and oppression disappear from the entire globe in our lifetime. We pray that the peoples of Mother Earth learn to negotiate, compromise, and work together to create a lasting peace. May we all live simply, so everyone can simply live healthy lives.

Passover

Passover refers to the night the Angel of Death passed over Jewish homes in Egypt in the Days of Moses.

May the Angel of Death pass over us all and keep us safe in dark times.

Passover is celebrated with the warmth and joy of a Seder, a ritual dinner shared with family and friends. We eat and drink together, sing songs, and tell the story of a people who were rescued from slavery. Tonight, we celebrate Freedom. We pray that one day soon all peoples will be safe and free.

Haggadah

This booklet is called a haggadah. "Haggadah" means, "to tell." It is the purpose of this Seder to tell the Passover story as God commanded. And so, year after year, we remember a time long ago when we were slaves. By remembering, may it help us to better appreciate our own freedom. It is a blessing, a mitzvah, to celebrate one of life's most precious gifts — freedom.

The Seder

This ritual dinner is called a "Seder." The word "Seder" means "order" because there is a set order to everything we do at a Seder. The table is set with special foods, each of which reminds us of some part of the Passover story.

As we look around, we see:
- candles
- haggadahs
- cups of wine
- Elijah's cup
- matzos plate
- special Seder plate.

(**Leader:** Lift up the Seder plate and point out each of the ritual foods on it.)

- karpas (a vegetable from Mother Earth)
- haroset (a sweet mixture of apples, nuts, raisins and cinnamon)
- salt water (for dipping eggs and karpas)
- a roasted egg
- a roasted bone
- morah (bitter herbs)
- wonderful wines

The symbolic meaning of each of these foods will be explained as we follow the haggadah and fulfill the blessed ritual of the Seder.

Candle Lighting

We sanctify each Sabbath and every sacred holiday by lighting the candles. Their flames are portals through which the Divine Forces of the Universe watch over us. As we light the candles, we invite our Holy Mother and our Holy Father to be present with us tonight.

Prayer for Kindling the Candles

Holy Mother, Holy Father, Eternal Sustainer of the Universe, we thank you for our well-being. Please watch over the world. We need your vigilance. Please seed a love of peace in the hearts of our leaders. Give them the wisdom and the patience to navigate safely through our current challenges. Send us strong men and women with vision and courage to guide us out of ignorance into a realm where Freedom reigns.

בָּרוּךְ אַתָּה יהוה אֱלֹהֵינוּ מֶלֶךְ הָעוֹלָם
אֲשֶׁר קִדְּשָׁנוּ בְּמִצְוֹתָיו וְצִוָּנוּ לְהַדְלִיק נֵר
שֶׁל (שַׁבָּת וְשֶׁל) יוֹם טוֹב.

Ba-ruch a-tah A-don-ai, El-o-hei-nu me-lech ha-olam, a-sher kidi-sha-nu b'mitz-vo-tav v'tzi-va-nu la-had-leek ner shel (Shab-bat va shel) yom tov.

The First Glass of Wine

(We dedicate this first cup of wine to:)
A suffering country, an ill relation, someone who has died, anyone in grief, someone who needs a blessing. Hold their names in your heart as we recite the following words together.

Eternal Guardian, we are all your children. Help us to recover from old wounds as we explore new avenues in this new time. We gladly open ourselves to love all the peoples on Mother Earth.

Let us lift our cups to recite the Kiddush over the first of four cups of wine. As we drink this first sacred glass of wine, we pray for all those in need.

קַדֵּשׁ

בָּרוּךְ אַתָּה יְיָ, אֱלֹהֵינוּ מֶלֶךְ הָעוֹלָם, בּוֹרֵא פְּרִי הַגָּפֶן:

Ba-ruch a-tah A-don-ai, El-o-hei-nu me-lech ha-olam, bo-ray pree ha-ga-fin.

On Shabbat add the words in brackets

בָּרוּךְ אַתָּה יְיָ, אֱלֹהֵינוּ מֶלֶךְ הָעוֹלָם, אֲשֶׁר בָּחַר בָּנוּ מִכָּל־עָם, וְרוֹמְמָנוּ מִכָּל־לָשׁוֹן, וְקִדְּשָׁנוּ בְּמִצְוֹתָיו, וַתִּתֶּן־לָנוּ יְיָ אֱלֹהֵינוּ בְּאַהֲבָה | שַׁבָּתוֹת לִמְנוּחָה וּ | מוֹעֲדִים לְשִׂמְחָה, חַגִּים וּזְמַנִּים לְשָׂשׂוֹן אֶת־יוֹם | הַשַּׁבָּת הַזֶּה וְאֶת - יוֹם | חַג הַמַּצּוֹת הַזֶּה. זְמַן חֵרוּתֵנוּ, | בְּאַהֲבָה, | מִקְרָא קֹדֶשׁ, זֵכֶר לִיצִיאַת מִצְרָיִם. כִּי בָנוּ בָחַרְתָּ וְאוֹתָנוּ קִדַּשְׁתָּ מִכָּל־הָעַמִּים. | וְשַׁבָּת | וּמוֹעֲדֵי קָדְשֶׁךָ | בְּאַהֲבָה וּבְרָצוֹן | בְּשִׂמְחָה וּבְשָׂשׂוֹן הִנְחַלְתָּנוּ: בָּרוּךְ אַתָּה יְיָ, מְקַדֵּשׁ | הַשַּׁבָּת וְ | יִשְׂרָאֵל וְהַזְּמַנִּים:

בָּרוּךְ אַתָּה יְיָ, אֱלֹהֵינוּ מֶלֶךְ הָעוֹלָם, שֶׁהֶחֱיָנוּ וְקִיְּמָנוּ וְהִגִּיעָנוּ לַזְּמַן הַזֶּה:

Ba-ruch a-tah A-don-ai, El-o-hei-nu me-lech ha-olam, a-sher b-char banu mikol—am, v-rom-manu mikol-lashon, v-kid-shanu b-mitz-vo-tav, va-ti-ten—lanu A-don-ai

Kaddush

El-o-hei-nu b-aha-vah (sha-ba-tot lim-nu-cha vu) moa-dim la-sim-ha cha-geem uz-man-im l-sa-son et—yom (ha-sha-bat ha-zeh v-et—yom) chag ha-matz-ot ha-zeh. Z-man cha-ru-tei-nu, (b-a-cha-vah,) meek-rah desh, za-cher lit-zi-at mitz-ra-yim. Ki va-nu va-char-ta v-au-tanu ki-dash-ta mi-kol ha-amin. (v-shab-bat) u-mo-a-die kad-shech (b-ah—ha-va uv-ra-tzon) b-sim-chah uv-sa-shon chan—chal-tanu.: Ba-ruch a-tah a-don-ai, m-ka-desh (ha-sha-bat v) yis-ra-eil v-haz-ma-nim. Ba-ruch a-tah A-don-ai, El-o-hei-nu me-lech ha-olam, she-che-chee-ya-nu v-ki-ma-nu vhig-ee-ah-nu liz-man ha-ze.

As we recall the journey from slavery to freedom, may each of us come to appreciate the freedom we enjoy. We are grateful to all those who valiantly sacrificed their lives for our freedom. We offer our heartfelt prayers for all who are not yet free. We pray that tyranny, poverty, hunger, and war will be eradicated in our lifetime.

We thank Mother Earth for the wine which adds joy to life and God for the mitzvas (blessings), which add holiness to life. We thank you Holy One, for making us holy through your commandments. In love, you have given us appointed times for gladness, festivals, and seasons of joy, which add beauty to our lives. This day is the Feast of Unleavened Bread, the season of our liberation. We join in love and holy gathering to remember the exodus from Egypt. You have given us the inheritance of love and benevolence, especially during sacred times. Blessed are you, O Lord, who makes Israel holy and has given us this festival season. Thank you O Shekhina, Mother of Life, for keeping us alive through all our challenges, so that we may find joy in what has come to us.

Hand Washing

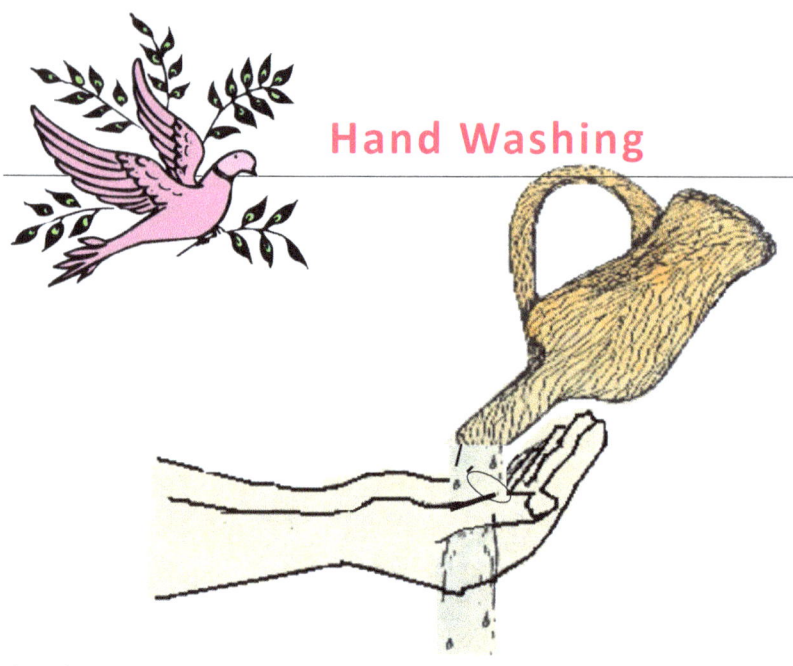

(Wash water will now be passed around. Please wash your hands in silence and do not speak until after we have recited the following prayer).

בָּרוּךְ אַתָּה יְיָ, אֱלֹהֵינוּ מֶלֶךְ הָעוֹלָם,
אֲשֶׁר קִדְּשָׁנוּ בְּמִצְוֹתָיו, וְצִוָּנוּ עַל נְטִילַת יָדָיִם.

Ba-ruch a-tah A-do-nai, El-o-hei-nu me-lech ha-olam, a-sher ki-dish-anu b-mitz-va-tanu v-tzi-va-nu ahl ne-ti-lat ya-die-um.

Karpas

We take a potato from the soil of Mother Earth and dip it in salt water. We are thankful for this gift of food in a world where so many are hungry. The salt water reminds us of the bitter tears shed by those who have too little to eat. They can survive their cruel ordeal because they dare to hope that one day they will be blessed as we have been. May the day come soon when all cruel bonds are broken and all people have plenty of healthy food to eat.

Dividing The Middle

(The leader uncovers the matzos and declares:)

Behold the matzos, bread of poverty, which our sisters and brothers have eaten in the lands of oppression.

We now break the middle matzah in two, one half is left under the cloth on the matzos plate. The other half becomes the afikomen, which will be hidden. After dinner, we will each eat a piece of the afikoman. Whoever finds the afikoman will receive a gift.

Hospitality

(The leader raises the Seder Plate and declares:)

Hospitality is always a mitzvah (a blessing), especially at Passover. We are told to open our hearts and make it possible for all who wish to do so, to observe the tradition of Passover at a Seder.

In the prayer which follows, we open our hearts to anyone who wishes to join in our celebration of freedom, peace, and love.

Please repeat after me: Behold all our relations. Let all who are hungry come eat. Let all who wish to share our abundance, come celebrate with us. Now many are still enslaved. Next year, may all peoples be free from hunger and oppression.

The Four Questions

(The youngest person present is given the honor of asking the four questions.)

1. Why is this night different from all other nights? On all other nights, we eat leavened or unleavened bread. Why on this night, do we eat only unleavened bread?
2. On all other nights, we eat all kinds of herbs. Why on this night, do we eat only bitter herbs?
3. On all other nights, we do not dip our vegetables even once. Why on this night, do we dip twice?
4. On all other nights, we eat either sitting or reclining. Why on this night, do we all recline?

מַה-נִּשְׁתַּנָּה הַלַּיְלָה הַזֶּה מִכָּל-הַלֵּילוֹת. שֶׁבְּכָל-הַלֵּילוֹת אָנוּ אוֹכְלִין חָמֵץ וּמַצָּה. הַלַּיְלָה הַזֶּה כֻּלוֹ מַצָּה.

שֶׁבְּכָל-הַלֵּילוֹת אָנוּ אוֹכְלִין שְׁאָר יְרָקוֹת. הַלַּיְלָה הַזֶּה מָרוֹר.

שֶׁבְּכָל-הַלֵּילוֹת אֵין אָנוּ מַטְבִּילִין אֲפִילוּ פַּעַם אֶחָת. הַלַּיְלָה הַזֶּה שְׁתֵּי פְעָמִים.

שֶׁבְּכָל-הַלֵּילוֹת אָנוּ אוֹכְלִין בֵּין יוֹשְׁבִין וּבֵין מְסֻבִּין. הַלַּיְלָה הַזֶּה כֻּלָּנוּ מְסֻבִּין.

1. Ma-nish-tana ha-lie-la ha-zeh mi-kol ha-lie-lot? Sheb-khol ha-lie-lot anu ok-lim kham-ets um matzos? Ha-lie-la ha-zeh kul matzos.
2. Sheb-khol ha-lie-lot anu ok-lim sh-ar yea-ra-kot; Ha-liela ha-zeh mar-or.
3. Sheb-khol ha-lie-lot anu mat-bil-lin ah-fee-lue pa-am ek-hot; Ha-liela ha-zeh sh-tie pa-ah-meem.
4. Sheb-khol ha-lie-lot anu ok-lim bein yo-shi-vin oo-veen miso-bean. Ha-liela ha-zeh ku-lanu miso-bean.

The Reply

This night is indeed different from all the other nights of the year. Through the foods we eat tonight, the rituals we perform, the songs we sing, and the prayers we offer, we seek to acknowledge our unity with all life and to rededicate ourselves to creating a world where freedom reigns for all.

Let us begin with your last question about reclining. We are seated on pillows in honor of our freedom. It is the way of slaves to eat hurriedly in fear. They eat standing up or squatting on the ground. Since this is the Festival of Freedom, we naturally eat in the manner of free men and women. Tonight, we are relaxed and unhurried as we give thanks for the abundance with which we are blessed.

If we had been born in another country or in another time, we too might ourselves be slaves today. As it is, there are still many in our family who are not yet free. Therefore, regardless of how wise we are, or how old we are, or how well we know the story, it is still a mitzvah (a blessing) and a duty to retell it tonight. The more we discuss the path to freedom, the more we come to understand the struggles everyone faces in their quest for peace.

The reason we eat unleavened bread, bitter herbs, and dip our vegetables in salt water, will all be made clear by the end of the Seder and so our story begins....

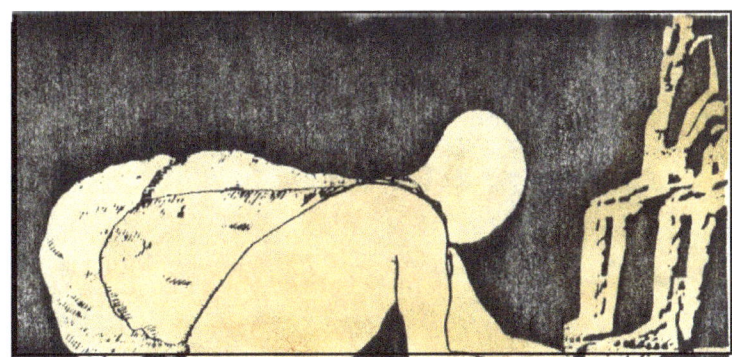

 # The Story of Passover

Turn Back the Clock

Our story begins a long time ago. Let us wend our way across the sands of time to a distant age in a foreign land. In ancient Canaan lived Joseph, a gifted child, the favorite son of Jacob. One day, Joseph's jealous brothers sold him to a passing caravan of Midianite merchants who took him to Egypt.

Pharaoh, the ruler of Egypt, had a strange dream. He saw seven lean cows emerge from the Nile and devour seven fat ones grazing near the river bank. Not a single wise man or wizard in all the land could find the meaning of this dream. Then Joseph, who had interpreted dreams for the royal cupbearer and baker, was called before the Pharaoh.

"I have dreamed a dream that no one in Egypt can interpret," said Pharaoh. Joseph answered, "God is the interpreter of dreams. Perhaps through me he shall grant the Pharaoh peace of mind."

Joseph listened and then told the Pharaoh that his dream prophesized seven years of famine would follow seven years of plenty throughout the land.

Joseph Becomes Governor

The Pharaoh rewarded the wise young Hebrew by appointing him governor over all Egypt. As the new governor, he built huge granaries and filled them during the years of plenty. When famine came, the full granaries saved Egypt from starvation.

During the famine, like many people from neighboring lands, Joseph's brothers came to Egypt to buy grain. The governor recognized them at once. Grateful for his own good fortune, Joseph saw their actions as destined by God and forgave them.

"Take as much grain as you need," he said, "and promise me that you will bring our father here so that he may spend his last years in this great land of plenty." Thus, the family was reunited and Jacob lived out his days with his beloved son.

A New Pharaoh

Many years passed. Generations came and went. Joseph and his good deeds were long forgotten. The new Pharaoh feared the Israelites for they had grown numerous over time, so he enslaved them.

Year after year, generation after generation, the children of Israel toiled under the taskmaster's whip. One day, the new Pharaoh had a dream. He saw an old man holding a set of scales in his hand. On one side was a small lamb and on the other side were all the great men of Egypt. The lamb outweighed them all.

Death to the Israelites

In the morning, one of the wise men interpreted Pharaoh's dream. He warned that the lamb represented the Israelites. A child would be born among them who would overthrow the throne of Egypt and set the Israelites free. The child would exceed all men in wisdom and his fame would be remembered forever.

In panic, Pharaoh commanded every baby boy born to the Israelites to be cast into the Nile. Thousands of children were drowned by this decree. There was great mourning and weeping among the Israelites.

There lived among the Israelites a man named Amram, of the tribe of Levi. When his wife Jocheved gave birth to a boy she hid him well, but Pharaoh sent spies to search for all newborn babies. Jocheved knew she could not keep her child hidden for long, so she made a cradle of bulrushes, the long reeds that grew at the river's edge, daubed it with pitch to make it waterproof, and laid the baby in the cradle. She blessed the basket and set it afloat down the Nile. Miriam, the baby's sister, protectively watched over the little basket from the river bank.

Rescued from the Nile

It happened that Thermuthis, daughter of Pharaoh, came to the river to bathe. She heard a child crying and rescued the little boy. Miriam bravely approached the princess and offered to call one of the Hebrew women to nurse the child. With the princess's permission, Miriam ran home to fetch her mother. And so it came to pass, little Moses was cared for by his own mother in the palace as an Egyptian prince, the son of Thermuthis.

Moses the Egyptian

Moses grew up in the palace of the Pharaoh and became a just man. He objected to the cruel enslavement of the Israelites. One day, he saw a guard beating an old man. He was so enraged by this injustice that he struck down the guard and buried him in the sand. When Pharaoh found out, he was furious and sentenced Moses to death!

Escape to Midian

Moses fled. When he came to a well in the land of Midian, where shepherd women were watering their flock, he met the seven daughters of Jethro. He graciously helped them and Zipporah, the eldest, invited the stranger to her father's tent. Moses married Zipporah and tended Jethro's flocks for many years.

And God Commanded Moses

When Moses was an elder, grazing his sheep near Mt. Sinai, he saw a fire spring up in a thorn bush. To his amazement, the bush was not consumed. Moses approached the bush. The booming voice of God called out to him from the fire, ordering him to remove his shoes for he was standing on sacred land. Then God commanded Moses to return to Egypt and set the children of Israel free.

Let my People Go

Let my People Go

When Israel was in Egypt's land,
Let my people go!
Oppressed so hard they could not stand,
Let my people go!

Go Down, Moses, way down in Egypt's land.
Tell old Pharaoh, Let my people go!

Thus saith the Lord, bold Moses said,
Let my people go!
If not I'll smite your people dead,
Let my people go!

Go Down, Moses, way down in Egypt's land.
Tell old Pharaoh, Let my people go!

As Israel stood by the water's side,
Let my people go!
By God's command it did divide,
Let my people go!

Go Down, Moses, way down in Egypt's land.
Tell old Pharaoh, Let my people go!

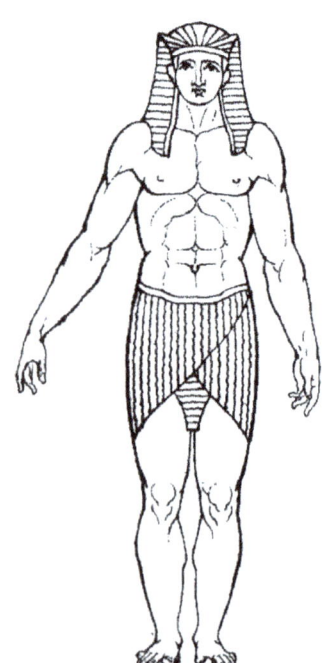

Confronting Pharaoh

Moses and his brother Aaron came before Pharaoh and asked him, in the name of the Unseen God, to free the Israelites. Pharaoh laughed and said he had never heard of such a god. Moses threw down his staff. It suddenly turned into a snake. Pharaoh laughed! His magicians could perform the same trick. Even though Moses' snake swallowed up all the others, Pharaoh remain unmoved.

Moses told Pharaoh that if he did not set the Israelites free, God would turn the waters of the Nile red with blood. The plague came as he foretold, but Pharaoh's heart remained hard. Then came one plague after another — a plague of frogs, of darkness, and of wild beasts. Each time, Pharaoh agreed to let the Israelites go free if only the plague would cease, and each time he refused to fulfill his promise.

The Last Plague

Then came the final plague that broke the will of Pharaoh. Death passed over the Jewish homes and struck every Egyptian first-born son. That night as Pharaoh's own son lay dying, he called Moses to him and demanded he take the Israelites out of Egypt. Moses gathered his people together and left in great haste. They baked unleavened bread because there was no time for the bread to rise. Thus, the first matzos were made.

The Ten Plagues of God

As we list the plagues that God unleashed upon the Egyptians, let us spill a drop of wine from our glasses. We do this to acknowledge our sorrow for their suffering. Our cup of joy cannot be full when we recall the suffering of the Egyptians.

Today many of our family still bleed and suffer under the tyranny of oppression. Just as we remember the past, let us also lament the present. We will also spill a drop of wine for each of those places in our present world where people are still oppressed and dying in their struggle to be free.

We pray for peace in:

- Blood
- Frogs
- Vermin
- Wild Beasts
- Cattle Disease
- Boils
- Hail
- Locusts
- Darkness
- Death of the First Born Son

- Israel
- Palestine
- Ukraine
- Libya
- Pakistan
- Syria
- South Sudan
- The Congo
- Afghanistan
- Nigeria

The story of the plagues contains a reminder and a warning to all nations. When they show no concern for human life and care nothing for human suffering, they are preparing for their own destruction. A nation that wants to grow and prosper must grant liberty and justice to all its inhabitants throughout the land.

The Israelites had been marching for three days when Pharaoh summoned his army and went in pursuit. With the Red Sea in front of them and the Egyptian army behind them, Moses prayed to God. The Lord parted the waters leaving dry land, so the Israelites could walk through. Pharaoh's army followed them into the sea. Once the Israelites reached the far shore, the water suddenly rushed back in swallowing the entire army. Only Pharaoh, watching from the riverbank was spared, so he might regret his injustice.

The Israelites wandered for forty years before they reached Canaan, the promised land beside the River Jordan. Along the way, on Mount Sinai, God gave Moses the Ten Commandments. In a land flowing with milk and honey, they began a new life, planted their vineyards, and harvested their crops.

Since those days, we have celebrated Passover on the first full moon in the spring. For eight days, we eat matzos to remind us of the unleavened bread our foremothers baked in haste as they fled Egypt.

Throughout the ages, Passover has celebrated the gift of freedom and promoted rebellion against oppression; whether it was escape from Egypt, from the Inquisition, the Crusades, or the Nazis, lovers of freedom have always overcome the bondage imposed upon them. This is the message we must keep alive in our hearts. Today, more than ever, we must value each person's right to be free.

The Four Children

Blessed be the Eternal who wisely reminds us that not all children are alike. Therefore, Passover needs to be presented in different ways to the wise child, the rebellious one, the simple one, and the little child too young to understand.

The Wise Child asks Curiously

"What is the meaning of the rules, laws, and customs which the Eternal has commanded us?" The wise child loves Passover and is eager to celebrate it. The parents should patiently explain all that there is to know about Passover and the worldwide struggle people have undergone and are still undergoing to be free. This child should learn not only how we observe the festival, but more importantly, why.

The Rebellious Child asks with Irritation

"Why do you do this old ritual year after year?"

Notice the child says, "you." He does not feel connected to the family and tradition holds no meaning for him. He feels separate, an outsider, alone. To such a child, the parents need to emphasize that we are all one family. They should say, "We observe this festival because of what God has done for us as we struggle towards our own freedom. Because our ancestors were freed from bondage, we are now free."

The Simple Child

The simple child asks, "What is this all about?"
Tell this child that we are grateful to the Eternal for bringing us out of slavery. Slavery is wrong. We must help all peoples to be free. Everyone deserves to be free.

The Young Child

The fourth child does not even know how to ask questions. Even when one does not know what to ask, a true teacher knows what to teach. Say simply, "This is a special night to celebrate the good things in our lives."

The Eggs

Let us take a boiled egg and dip it in salt water. The egg symbolizes fertility and new life. It is spring and hope is born anew. May the struggles of past winters be left behind as we rejoice with new hope for a healthy, cooperative world where everyone is free.

(The leader asks:)

What shall be birthed anew on Mother Earth?

(Everyone answers:)
* Peaceful strategies for living.
* A cooperative paradigm based on mutual respect.
* A foundation for a lasting peace.
* Creative solutions for healing the many wounds of the world.

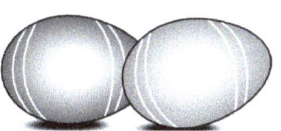

Dayeynu

Dayeynu (pronounced dy-ey-nu) means – it is enough for us. It is a way of looking at life and being satisfied with what you have.
This song is a list of our blessings.

If God had brought us out of Egypt
But not split the Red Sea for us, dayeynu
Dy-dy-eynu-oo, dy-dy-eynu-oo, dy-dy-eynu, dy-eynu-dy-eynu.

If God had given us the Sabbath
But not built the Holy Temple, dayeynu.
Dy-dy-eynu-oo, dy-dy-eynu-oo, dy-dy-eynu, dy-eynu-dy-eynu.

If God had given us the Torah
But not brought of us into Israel, dayeynu.
Dy-dy-eynu-oo, dy-dy-eynu-oo, dy-dy-eynu, dy-eynu-dy-eynu.

When there's food for one and all
And each child is safe at home, dayeynu.
Dy-dy-eynu-oo, dy-dy-eynu-oo, dy-dy-eynu, dy-eynu-dy-eynu.

Soon all wars will no more
And one world we'll be again, dayeynu.
Dy-dy-eynu-oo, dy-dy-eynu-oo, dy-dy-eynu, dy-eynu-dy-eynu.
Dy-dy-eynu-oo, dy-dy-eynu-oo, dy-dy-eynu, dy-eynu-dy-eynu.

The Seder Plate

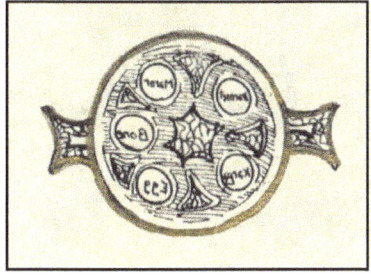

(The leader raises the Seder Plate, points to the roasted bone and asks:)

Why do we have a roasted bone on the Seder Plate?

(Everyone answers:)
The roasted bone is here to remind us that humanity has sacrificed enough tender young lambs. Enough people have suffered and died. If we want to remain free, we must help all people to be free, and we must be ready to grant the same freedom to all people.

Maror

(The leader points to the maror and asks:)

Why do we eat bitter herbs?

(Everyone answers:)
The maror is bitter, as is our sadness. Five thousand years have passed, and all our people are not yet free. When we eat the maror, we taste the bitterness of slavery, poverty, illness, war, hunger, and despair.

Haroset

(The leader points to the Haroset and asks:)

Why do we eat sweet haroset?

(Everyone answers:)
Har-o-set represents the mortar, the clay and the blood of the slaves who labored to build the pyramids. The haroset is as sweet as the dream of our children living together in a safe cooperative world.

The Matzos

(The leader lifts the matzos plate and asks:)

Why do we eat matzos on Passover?

(Everyone answers:)

The matzos are here to remind us that poverty and oppression still exist. When we eat this dry bread, let us remember those who still have too little to eat. Just as the Israelites did not tarry in their flight to freedom, so too, we must not delay in helping whomever we can to overcome hunger and attain lasting freedom.

Khazeret

(The leader points to the khazeret and asks:)

Why is the khazeret here?

(Everyone answers:)

The lettuce starts out sweet, but if it is left in the ground too long, it becomes bitter. When people are oppressed, they too can become bitter.

The Second Cup of Wine

(Please lift your cup.)

In each generation there are those who love unquestioningly. They give all they can to nurture and help people through difficult times. We raise our cups and give thanks to all those who have helped us along the way. We pray that a passionate flame of peace will soon light the world and many paths will appear that teach us how to creatively live together. May the world experience the same quality of freedom, joy, and peace that we are sharing here tonight.

God promised our ancestors that He would not let them be annihilated. With this cup of wine, we now promise our children, and our children's children, that we will do whatever we can to preserve the quality of life on this beautiful planet.

(While holding your cups, please recite together:)

בָּרוּךְ אַתָּה יְיָ, אֱלֹהֵינוּ מֶלֶךְ הָעוֹלָם,
בּוֹרֵא פְּרִי הַגָּפֶן.

Ba-ruch a-tah A-donai, El-o-hei-nu me-lech ha-olam, bo-ra pree ha-ga-fen.

Blessed are you, Holy Mother Shekhina, Guardian of the Universe, She who created the fruit of the vine.

Hillel Sandwich

(Break the top and middle matzos into pieces. Give each guest two pieces of matzah. Put some maror and some haroset between the two pieces of matzos. This is called a Hillel Sandwich. Hillel was a scholar and a very wise man. Let us all recite the following blessing together.)

בָּרוּךְ אַתָּה יְיָ, אֱלֹהֵינוּ מֶלֶךְ הָעוֹלָם,
הַמּוֹצִיא לֶחֶם מִן־הָאָרֶץ.

Ba-ruch a-tah A-donai, El-o-hei-nu me-lech ha-olam, ha-moi-ze le-chem min ha-ar-etz.

Blessed are you, Holy Mother Shekhina, who brings forth the wheat from the earth. May all who hunger have enough food to eat.

Holy Mother, Holy Father, I am eating the bitter with the sweet. I am grateful for the simple bread of survival. Please bless my hands and help me to be a source of nourishment to the world around me. Guide me as I work to make my world a healthier place. Amen.

Dinner is served.

After Dinner the Ritual Continues

The Third Cup of Wine

On our Seder table there is a cup of wine from which no one has drunk. It is reserved for a special guest — the prophet Elijah.

The Bible recalls many wonderful stories about Elijah. He was a man of great courage who fought for what was just and right.

According to tradition, Elijah never died. He rose into heaven. One day, he will return to Earth to herald the arrival of a time when all people will live together in peace, a time when people will treat each other with kindness and respect.

Elijah was a champion of those in need, those burdened by troubles. He performed miracles to help people in danger and was a bringer of hope and joy.

Legend tells us that on Passover, Elijah visits every Seder and sips a little wine from his cup.

(Please open the door and welcome Elijah into our home.)
(Let us lift the third cup of wine and recite the blessing.

בָּרוּךְ אַתָּה יְיָ, אֱלֹהֵינוּ מֶלֶךְ הָעוֹלָם,
בּוֹרֵא פְּרִי הַגָּפֶן.

Ba-ruch a-tah A-donai, El-o-hei-nu me-lech ha-olam, bo-ra pree ha-ga-fen.

Afikomon

Now that we have eaten. we are ready to complete the ritual. Where is the afikoman? It will be divided among the guests and eaten in a reclining position. (Exchange it for a gift to the child/children who found it.)

Blessings

(The Torah tells us: When you have eaten and are satisfied, give thanks. Let us now join in expressing our gratitude for the many blessings in our lives. Please repeat each prayer after me.)

"Blessed are you, Holy Mother, Holy Father, Guardians of Humanity,

We thank you for the goodness in the world that sustains us."

"We thank you for all the acts of mercy and loving kindness that we have received and have been blessed to perform."

"We thank you for the opportunities we have had to share our good fortune with those in need."

"We thank you for all the kind people who are feeding the hungry children in the world."

"We thank you for all the brave people who are working to end these wasteful wars and liberate the oppressed."

"We thank you for all the great visionaries who embody sacredness and peace."

"We thank you for the holy land of Israel and for all the compassionate people who are working to resolve deep-seeded differences. Bless those who are striving to create a lasting peace and will one day bring liberty to all the people living in the holy land."

Let us end with a silent blessing of your own.

The Fourth Cup of Wine

(Please lift the fourth cup of wine and together we recite the blessing.)

בָּרוּךְ אַתָּה יְיָ, אֱלֹהֵינוּ מֶלֶךְ הָעוֹלָם,
בּוֹרֵא פְּרִי הַגָּפֶן.

Ba-ruch a-tah A-donai, El-o-hei-nu me-lech ha-olam, bo-ra pree ha-ga-fen.

Jerusalem

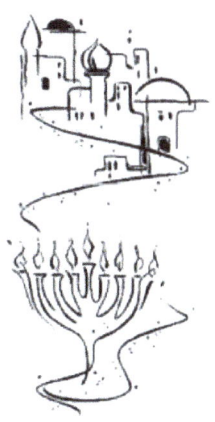

As we come to the end of our Seder, we pray that we may all celebrate together again next year in good health, joy, and freedom. Next year, may Jerusalem be the spiritual center of a peaceful world.

Had Gadya

(This song is sung faster and faster as it goes on:)

An only kid! An only kid!
My father bought for two Zuzim. **Had gad-ya, had gad-ya.**

Then came a cat that ate the kid,
My father bought for two Zuzim. **Had gad-ya, had gad-ya.**

Then came a dog, that bit the cat, that ate the kid,
My father bought for two Zuzim. **Had gad-ya, had gad-ya.**

Then came a stick, that beat the dog,
That bit the cat, that ate the kid,
My father bought for two Zuzim. **Had gad-ya, had gad-ya.**

Then came a fire, that burned the stick,
That beat the dog, that bit the cat,
That ate the kid,
My father bought for two Zuzim. **Had gadya, had gadya.**

Then came the water, that quenched the fire,
That burned the stick, that beat the dog,
That bit the cat, that ate the kid,
My father bought for two Zuzim. **Had gad-ya, had gad-ya.**

Then came the ox, that drank the water,
That quenched the fire, that burned the stick,
That beat the dog, that bit the cat, that ate the kid,
My father bought for two Zuzim. **Had gad-ya, had gad-ya.**

Then came a man, who slew the ox, that drank the water,
That quenched the fire, that burned the stick, that beat the dog,
That bit the cat, that ate the kid,
My father bought for two Zuzim. **Had gad-ya, had gad-ya.**

Then came The Angel of Death, who took the man,
Who slew the ox, that drank the water, that quenched the fire,
That burned the stick, that beat the dog, that bit the cat,
That ate the kid,
My father bought for two Zuzim. **Had gad-ya, had gad-ya.**

Then came the Eternal, Blessed Guardian,
Who smote the Angel of Death, who took the man, who slew the ox,
That drank the water, that quenched the fire,
That burned the stick, that beat the dog,
That bit the cat, that ate the kid,
My father bought for two Zuzim. **Had gad-ya, had gad-ya.**

Martin Luther King

"I have a dream that my four children will one day live in a nation where they will not be judged by the color of their skin, but by the content of their character. I have a dream today. I have a dream that one day every village shall be exalted, every hill and mountain shall be made low, the rough places will be made plain, and the glory of the Lord shall be revealed, and all flesh will see it together.

"This shall be the day when all of God's children will be able to sing with new meaning, 'My country 'tis of thee, sweet land of liberty, of thee I sing. Land where my fathers died, land of the pilgrims' pride, from every mountainside, let freedom ring.'

"So, let freedom ring from the prodigious hilltops of New Hampshire! Let freedom ring from the mighty mountains of New York! Let freedom ring from the heightening Alleghenies of Pennsylvania! Let freedom ring from the snowcapped Rockies of Colorado! Let freedom ring from the curvaceous peaks of California! But not only that. Let freedom ring from Stone Mountain Georgia! Let freedom ring from every hill and mole hill in Mississippi! From every mountainside, let freedom ring!

"When we let freedom ring, when we let it ring from every village and every hamlet, from every state and every city, we shall be able to speed up that day when all of God's children, Black and White, Jews and Gentiles, Protestants and Catholics, (Muslims and Americans) will be able to join hands and sing in the words of that old Negro spiritual —

(All say together:)

**Free at last! Free at last!
May all Earth's children be free at last!**

In loving memory of
Charles and Bodhi Bebeau

Designed and Produced by
N*I*N Sharyn Bebeau

www.ingramcontent.com/pod-product-compliance
Lightning Source LLC
Chambersburg PA
CBHW060520300426
44112CB00017B/2740